Heroes for Young Readers

Written by Renee Taft Meloche
Illustrated by Bryan Pollard

Gladys Aylward
Corrie ten Boom
William Carey
Amy Carmichael
Jim Elliot
Jonathan Goforth
Betty Greene
Adoniram Judson
Eric Liddell
David Livingstone
Lottie Moon
George Müller
Nate Saint
Mary Slessor
Hudson Taylor
Cameron Townsend

…and more coming soon.

Heroes for Young Readers are based on the *Christian Heroes: Then & Now* biographies by Janet and Geoff Benge. Don't miss out on these exciting, true adventures for ages ten and up! See the back of this book for a full listing of the biographies loved by children, parents, and teachers.

For a free catalog of books and materials contact
YWAM Publishing, P.O. Box 55787, Seattle, WA 98155
1-800-922-2143, www.ywampublishing.com

HEROES FOR YOUNG READERS

JONATHAN GOFORTH

Never Give Up

Written by Renee Taft Meloche
Illustrated by Bryan Pollard

P.O. BOX 55787 SEATTLE, WA 98155

Jonathan Goforth: Never Give Up Text © 2004 by Renee Taft Meloche Illustrations © 2004 by Bryan Pollard
Published by YWAM Publishing, P.O. Box 55787, Seattle, WA 98155 ISBN 1-57658-242-6 Printed in China. All rights reserved.

A young man bound for college sat
    inside a speeding train.
He peered outside his window at
    the rolling green terrain.

His name was Jonathan Goforth.
    In eighteen eighty-three
he headed for the city of
    Toronto eagerly.

Raised on a farm in Canada,
    he'd worked hard and was strong,
yet felt a little nervous as
    his train rattled along.

At home he had ten siblings and
    his parents were quite poor.
He'd never seen a city, much
    less lived in one before.

He planned to go to college so
    that he could work for God
by preaching in another land,
    a place far-off, abroad.

Since all the other students would
    be Christians just like him,
he hoped that he would be well liked
    and that he would fit in.

But soon he was surprised by something
    he did not expect:
a farm boy among city boys
    was not given respect.

A classmate taunted, others laughed,
    "Just look at that boy's suit!
His mama must have made it for
    him; doesn't he look cute?"

As Jonathan, embarrassed, did
    not know how to respond,
he noticed for the first time what
    fine clothes they all had on.

They wore expensive tailored suits,
    unlike the clothes he owned.
He went back to his room and sat
    in silence—all alone.

He bought some fabric with a little
     money he had left.
He soon would have a tailored suit
     and be dressed like the rest.

He took the fabric to his room,
     where much to his surprise,
his classmates barged right in on him
     with cold, unfriendly eyes.

They took a rope and tied him—they
     were rough and they were quick—
then took his fabric and with scissors
     hacked a hole in it.

They put the cloth over his head
    and spun him round and round
until he found it hard to walk
    and not land on the ground.

They carried him outside his room
and stood him on the floor.
They made him try to walk, though dizzy,
down the corridor.

His classmates lined the hall and kicked
and pushed him to and fro
till they grew tired of their game,
unbound him, let him go.

Since he was poor and from a farm,
    his classmates had been mean,
but Jonathan was sure that he
    could not give up his dream.

Determined, he would stay and study
    hard till school was done
so he could sail to other lands
    and teach about God's Son.

As Jonathan continued school,
    he visited the slums—
so full of danger that most other
    Christians dared not come.

He visited the prison, too,
    and took the time to tell
the prisoners about God's love
    inside their tiny cells.

A deep respect and admiration
    grew for Jonathan.
His courage and his kindness made
    his classmates, one by one,
apologize for how they had
    behaved when he first came.
They'd thought he was not good enough
    and now they felt ashamed.

Soon Jonathan felt he should go—
    once he got his degree—
to China, where too few had heard
    of Christianity.

And soon his classmates came to him
    and said, "We have agreed
to help support you when you go
    and give you what you need."

As Jonathan stood speechless, his
    blue eyes filled up with tears.
These men who once had mocked him would
    now bless him through the years.

Upon his graduation, though,
    he could not leave just yet,
for first he married Rosalind,
    an artist whom he'd met.

They left for China and arrived
    in eighteen eighty-eight.
They learned the Chinese language so
    they could communicate.

They traveled into China and
they built a home of wood.
The Chinese came to visit, which
made both of them feel good.

The Chinese loved the music box
that Rosalind brought along—
an organ that she played for them
while singing Bible songs.

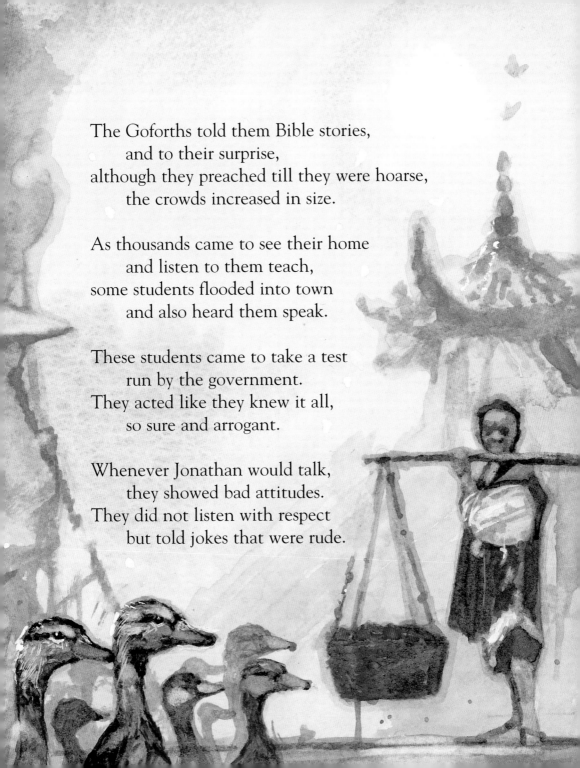

The Goforths told them Bible stories,
    and to their surprise,
although they preached till they were hoarse,
    the crowds increased in size.

As thousands came to see their home
    and listen to them teach,
some students flooded into town
    and also heard them speak.

These students came to take a test
    run by the government.
They acted like they knew it all,
    so sure and arrogant.

Whenever Jonathan would talk,
    they showed bad attitudes.
They did not listen with respect
    but told jokes that were rude.

So Jonathan—not one to quit—
    thought of a plan one day.
He got a globe and put it in
    his study on display.

"What's that big ball?" a student asked,
    and Jonathan replied,
"That's what the earth looks like," and then
    another student cried,
"It cannot be! We all know that
    the earth is very flat.
If it were round we would fall off
    the bottom—just like that!"

The students laughed at Jonathan
though he had just begun;
he told them how the earth can turn
and move around the sun.

He spoke of gravity and things
they had not heard before.
Amazed at this new science, they
all clamored to learn more.

He answered all their questions and
then turned the conversation
to God, the Bible, and its truths
for their consideration.

The students kept returning; their
    respect increased a lot
for Jonathan and all the new,
    intriguing things he taught.

Some students became Christians and
    soon spread the news around.
They told about the one true God
    in villages and towns.

Soon fifty groups of Christians met—
    among them one young man
who knew that when he told his dad
    he would not understand.

His father disliked Christians, yet
    this son went bravely home
to say, "I know the Christian God
    and follow Him alone."

Days later this young man showed up
        back at the Goforths' place.
His clothes were shredded, and he had
        been beaten in the face.

As Jonathan helped wash his wounds,
        he said, "My father kicked me,
and then I hid beneath some straw
        till it was safe to flee."

Then Jonathan, with kindness, said,
        "I'll visit in your town.
Your father must be quite upset.
        I'll try to calm him down."

He walked for many miles with other
     Christians the next day.
When they arrived, the Chinese there
     did not want them to stay.

The father would not meet, so in
     the streets they preached out loud,
but no one came and so they sang
     some hymns to draw a crowd.

The Chinese, one by one, approached
     and listened to their songs.
And soon the two groups, over tea,
     began to get along.

In time a few accepted that
    the Word of God is true,
and almost all the young man's family
    soon believed it too.

And once the father saw the difference
    in his family's lives,
he too became a Christian, much
    to everyone's surprise.

No longer did he curse, but sang
    out songs to praise his Lord.
No longer were the children frightened
    by him anymore.

Instead he now was kind to them,
    and when he saw his son,
he said, "Go help the Christians in
    the work they have begun.
For others need to hear about
    this God and understand
He is so great that He has changed
    this old and angry man."

When Jonathan was seventy-three
    he fully lost his vision.
Though blind, he kept on working at
    his lifelong teaching mission.

For he knew much by memory
    of the New Testament.
He traveled, preaching to great crowds
    of people where he went.

When he returned to Canada,
    he spoke most urgently.
He told the Christians, "We need your
    help working overseas.
The opportunity to spread
    the Word," he said, "is great,
and if you feel that you can work
    in missions, please don't wait."

He spoke in churches everywhere.
    His time was in demand.
He kept inspiring others till
    his death in his homeland.

Though Jonathan knew ridicule,
    mockery, and spite,
he did not quit; instead he did
    what God's Word says is right.

Like him, we should not give in when
    life seems unfair and cruel,
but live our lives with confidence
    in God's love and His rule.

Christian Heroes: Then & Now

by Janet and Geoff Benge

Heroes of History

by Janet and Geoff Benge

...and more coming soon. Unit study curriculum guides are also available.

For a free catalog of books and materials contact
YWAM Publishing, P.O. Box 55787, Seattle, WA 98155
1-800-922-2143, www.ywampublishing.com